MARY!

HOPE GETS
BACK UP —
every time!

ANA CHRISTINA

Dedicated to those whose
hearts are called to help others.

To those who serve.
To those who help us heal.
To those who lift us up.

Thank you.

"Whatever you think you can do or
believe you can do,
begin it.
Action has magic, grace, and
power in it."
Johann Wolfgang von Goethe

Oh my Strength,
I watch for You.
Though I may sit in darkness,
You will be my light;
though I have fallen,
I will rise.
Inspired by Ps. 59:9 & Micah 7:8

Burnout's Kryptonite

3 Simple Tools to Stop Burnout
(before burnout stops you)

ANA-CHRISTINA HICKS
Specialist—Simple Resilience Tools
Career Resilience Coach | Speaker | Trainer
www.toolsofhope.com

Table of Contents
Enjoy Enjoy, you Crazy-Awesome you!

Oh, to thrill in the moment.
To love openly.
To cry with honesty.
To live with eyes of wonder.
To laugh with abandon.
To feel delight in your soul.
This I wish for you.

Love, joy, patience, peace. Bless you.
Bless the work of your hands.
Love, *ANA-CHRISTINA*

Welcome!

If you have the heart of a helper, you know what it's like to do all you can, and still feel that it's not enough. If you have the heart of a helper, regardless of your chosen field, you know that it can be all-too-easy to burn out.

If you have people who count on you, you are a "emergency responder" to them, aren't you? In our personal lives—with our children, our spouse, our family, our friends, our colleagues—we often find ourselves helping out in the emergencies of life. If you've ever gotten the panic call, or the emergency call from a loved one, you were here for them in that moment.

If you have the heart of a helper, it means you have a gift and passion for providing aid. You serve others. You lift others. You support others.

My question is—**who is there to support you**?

Burnout's Kryptonite, the class, and this book were developed after hundreds of conversations with people who do emergency response for a living.

Here's a shout-out and thank-you to the helpers!

It's time to stop burnout. Let's get going.

Build Rock-Solid Confidence

UpYourGame RaiseYourHappy GetYourLifeBack

High-stress, demanding role? Stuck? Burned out?

Feeling lost?

Think you should have "figured it out" by now?

Tired and burned out by life?

I get it.

As a single mom whose life was reshaped by violence, I lost myself in the need to take care of everyone and everything else.

There was a point at which I couldn't do it anymore.

My whole body was hurting. Doctors and medicine couldn't find solutions for the chronic symptoms I had. I was unhappy at work. Unhappy at home. I was lost and empty.

I needed a change.

Simple choices. Simple shifts. Simple tools.

I went from burned-out corporate professional to happy, healthy, hopeful, and making a difference.

How? That's the beautiful part.

Through some traumatic experiences, I met first responders up close. I was inspired by their resilience in the midst of misery. I wanted to know how they made that work.

Trauma happens.

Stuck happens.

RESILIENCE HAPPENS.

My passion for sharing these tools began when I started providing resilience training for emergency responders. Professionally, I assumed they would be my target audience. What is intriguing to me is that my resilience tools are regularly requested and utilized across a wide spectrum of occupations; from government employees to chaplains, from corporate bankers to victim advocates, from military personnel to teachers, from district attorney staff to administrative personnel, from coaches and counselors to sales and customer service teams.

Helping professionals, all. Battling through because even though they want to make a difference, they are feeling lost, empty, and burned out. They want instant resets so that they can think clearly again.

This isn't pie in the sky, 20,000 feet in the air, vague, "be happy" motivational speaking – even though you may very well find it to be motivating.

It's based on my resilience coaching process. It's not counselling. It's not week-after-week dredging up past history. It's not airing dirty laundry.

Instead… it's real-life, simple-to-use tools to move forward into the life you REALLY want.

With the right tools, it's possible to change in a moment.

my moment becomes my minute becomes my hour becomes my day becomes my week becomes my month becomes my year becomes my life. my

live. your.

moment bec

becomes my day becomes my week becomes my

month beco

moment.

moment bec

becomes my day becomes my week becomes my

month becomes my year becomes my life. my

moment becomes my minute becomes my hour

becom

live. your. life.

mont

moment becomes my minute becomes my hour

becomes my day becomes my week becomes my

month becomes my year becomes my life.

TOOLS
of HOPE

Burnout Stinks

My life had become a nightmare and no one knew.

I was stuck. I was living on a tiny Alaskan island in the middle of the Bering Sea.

I had three small boys, my marriage was a disaster, and I was being viciously attacked by the man who had promised to love me.

The relationship had devolved over a period of years and now it was worse than ever. It was emotionally and mentally abusive. Things got turned around and always seemed to be my fault. I was berated and blamed. I was told I was crazy. I could never do anything right. It was physically abusive as well. I was struck, head-butted, thrown to the ground, strangled, and threatened with increasing regularity.

My thoughts were tangled, confused. I felt anguish in my soul. I remember it was like some sort of sick, sick mantra that I would think over and over, "I don't know how much longer I can do this."

> Do you ever get to the point where you think:
> **"I don't know how much longer I can do this."**

There were no mental health services on the island. There were 600 permanent residents at the time (Imagine: super small town. Two main dirt roads. Only way off was by cargo ship, fishing boat, or plane.)

I was ashamed, embarrassed, and humiliated to know that I was living like this. I was smarter than this. How had I gotten so dumb? I felt so trapped. The mental, emotional and physical toll were taking more than I had to give. I was hopeless, felt helpless, and was scrabbling with all that was in me to keep from falling into total despair.

I didn't have enough money to get off the island, he'd hidden the return plane tickets, and I was losing all of my energy for living.

In the end, it was my love for my children that saved me. I didn't want them to continue to have this role model of a man in their lives.

God provided a way out. There was a woman who moved to the island for only one year. It turns out that it was the year I needed help. Through the grapevine, I heard she used to be a counselor even though she wasn't working in that field anymore. When I had reached my breaking point, I reached out.

She listened, asked me questions, and taught me about boundaries. I had never known about them or how to set them or use them. I had been numb and in denial. After a long, very serious conversation, I knew were in more danger than I had realized.

With her help, I planned an escape. At that time, only three flights were scheduled per week. They were very often cancelled due to unsafe weather conditions or high wind warnings.

It was a last-minute, carefully planned escape. I was in fight or flight for two days leading up to it. Carefully controlled panic, if there is such a thing. Thank God the plane landed that day. We escaped on a Saturday morning and landed in Denver on Sunday afternoon, after a red-eye flight and a total of four layovers.

Thrilled to be there, safe. Stunned and filled with a kind of bittersweet shock, hardly able to take in how fast it had all happened.

I know what it's like to be knocked down.
I know what it's like to scrape myself up off the floor.
I know what it's like to start over with only the clothing on our backs. Thank God for those who helped us in those first few weeks and months.

Years later, I knew it was time to start sharing the tools that helped me get back up. As I helped others, I learned more and more.

Ever feel like you're stuck in a deep dark hole, with life raining down on you, stuck between a rock and a hard place?

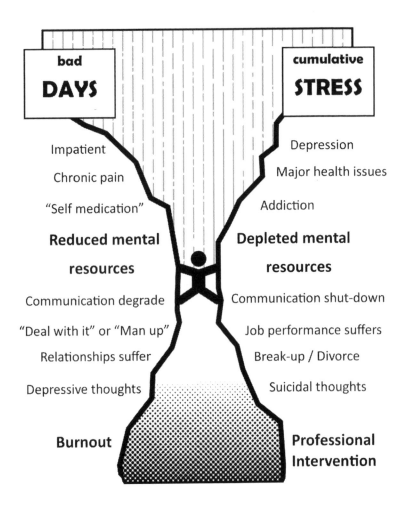

Stuck in the gap between boring and drama?
Stuck with feelings of emptiness and frustration?
Stuck with self-sabotage, stress, and bad days?

Do any of these look uncomfortably familiar?

* You losing **sleep** over your worries?
* Are you gaining / losing **weight** from stress?
* **Impatient** with your family?
* Growing **cynical**? Less compassionate?
* Is your job negatively impacting your **health**?
* Financial issues weighing you down?
* Is your stress hurting your **relationships**?

Ever feel like your work is taking all you have?

No one taught you how to deal with the all the stress, all at once, did they?

How many classes filled with rules, regulations, protocols, management, leadership, math, science and technical specialties did you take?

Ok. Now...

How many classes taught you how to go home to be with your loved ones after being a part of someone else's worst day? Hours of people hurting? Hours of people complaining? Tough days where you felt like all you had was not nearly enough?

How many classes taught you to deal with the pain you see or hear daily?

How many of those classes taught you to come home and be able to drop the stress when you hit your front door so that you can be present for yourself and your loved ones?

How many classes taught you how to deal everything happening all at the same time? (Work, relationship, kiddos, aging parents, no friends, poor friends, not enough time to hang with friends, health issues, poor sleep, etc.) **All at once! Not enough time! No rest for the unsung heroes!**

Most of my clients laugh, and say, "Zero" or "None."

You haven't gotten the tools. If you relax, you'll find this to be an easy, fun, and powerful process.

It's not your fault that you didn't get the training. You may not have gotten the tools at the beginning of your career, and it's not too late to get effective tools now, regardless of how many years it's been.

I've talked to hundreds of professionals in demanding roles.

There are patterns that come up in the conversations. You are not alone in your doubts and fears.

"Why do I keep doing the same thing over & over?"
"Why can't I seem to get ahead?"
"Why do I keep repeating the same mistakes?"
"I don't want to seem weak so I hold it all in."

Fear of not being enough.
Fear of not doing enough.
Fear of never having enough.
Fear of not being worth enough.
Fear of not being accepted.
Fear of failure.
Fear of not being loved.
Fear of never being good enough... ever.

It's important to know that others are struggling with some of the same things, isn't it? Even more important, to know **that there are people out there making it work.** There are ways. There are tools.

Not sure about you, but I want those kinds of tools.

It's time.

Trade self-doubt for peace and patience.

Trade self-sabotage for joy and love.

Trade stuck for freedom.

GetYourLifeBack.

26   Burnout's Kryptonite

The Birth of Burnout's Kryptonite

There is a way to live Radically Resilient. There is a way to Build Rock-Solid Confidence. There is a way to start LIVING your life.

There is a way to be happy and do work that is satisfying. There is a way to put it into perspective – even on the worst days.

There is a way to carry the job differently.

Even after a bad day. Even after bad meetings. Even after bad calls. Even after bad conversations. *Even after you've tried everything else.* There are options. It is possible to thrive in a tough job that uses your gifts, skills and training. When you are resilient, you will save enough energy to make another choice if and when that's needed. Powerful.

The original presentation, Burnout's Kryptonite, was birthed from conversations with hundreds of first responders from across the country.

Over and over, they would share the pain and the triumphs of their jobs. Call after call, responding to emergencies day after day. Seeing, hearing and feeling the misery, pain and loss of others. When I found out that many first responders (fire, police, EMS, 911 dispatch, victim advocates) have terrible stress statistics, I dearly wanted to help.

I wanted a way to give back. How do you help the helpers? I wanted to know their biggest pain points so that we could "kryptonite" them.

We have to identify the pain in order to disable it and start to heal, don't we?

I attended first responder conferences all over the country, not as a speaker, but as an audience member. I took as many classes as I possible. I talked to as many first responders as I could. When I asked them about their biggest challenges, they told me.

When I reviewed my notes and conversations, what they wanted was **quick resets** between bad calls. They said being able to reset quicker would help them deal with the emotional weight of their work and the toll it takes on them, their health, their relationships.

They told me that a successful reset would allow them to think more clearly, respond more appropriately, and recover more quickly.

> Results of a quick reset:
> Think more clearly.
> Respond more appropriately.
> Be less stressed overall.

As I looked deeper into hundreds of pages of notes, three themes emerged. They wanted to be more successful in their work. They wanted to be happier. They wanted to get their personal lives back.

That's a big part of what you want, isn't it? Can you imagine what your life will be like when you are more successful, happier, and when you're living the life you have always wanted?

Ultimately, from that information, I sought simple, practical tools that would create instant resets. I developed a presentation using those tools.
Hello, Burnout's Kryptonite.

UpYourGame
RaiseYourHappy
GetYourLifeBack

It doesn't matter what your work is—you could use some of this, couldn't you?

I have talked to many who feel called to serve others and yet find themselves deeply unhappy because of the stress.

You might not be experiencing this right now, but have you ever felt like your calling is killing you?

"I've helped all these people today but I'm dying inside."

I work with many professionals who are concerned with their health, frustrated with their finances, or struggling with the impact that a demanding career has on their relationships.

Argh. Struggling not only with **tough days, day after day**, but your own health, money, relationship, family, aging parents, and self-confidence issues.

And? Let's not forget.
Feeling alone while dealing with real, painful issues. Facing problems that you don't think you can share with anyone. Thinking you *"should"* know how to fix this, but you're not sure how.

When you're a helper, it can be so hard to be the one to ask for help.

You wouldn't happen to know anyone like that, would you? ;)

I am a resilience coach and speaker. I've had hundreds of great conversations with audience members. Sometimes it's sad. Sometimes triumphant. Sometimes it's super funny. Always, it's interesting.

When I work with first responder or military audiences, they often ask questions about my history.
"Have you been a cop?"
Me, "Nope."
"Are you in fire?"
Me, "Nope."
"You a medic?"
Me, "Nope."
"You dispatch?"
Me, "Nope."
"Military?"
Me, "Nope."
At that point, sometimes the more direct ones ask, "Well, then why {in the h***} are you here then?"

When I work with business and corporate audiences, they ask me similar questions:
You an accountant? Nope.
You been in banking? Nope.
You have medical training? Nope.
Have you worked in education? Nope.
You been in management? Yes!

More love. More peace.
More patience. More joy.
More LIFE. More More More.

The world needs you.
The world needs your gifts.
The world needs your uniqueness.

The fact is that sometimes the past gets in the way.

Unfortunate truth? I had lived a nightmare. We escaped a nightmare. **I lived bitter and unforgiving for seven years after we escaped.** I was mad. Hurt. So bitter. Oh-so-bitter. I was closed off and shut down as a mom. I was an angry, guarded colleague. I hid myself and my feelings from my family members. <u>Not proud of that time in my life</u>.

Nope. Not so proud at all.

Seven years I can never get back. Seven years that are lost and can't be re-lived.

And yet, we do the best we can do with the tools we have available to us, don't we?

We fight. We get scrappy. We survive day-to-day.

Let's get real.

We don't simply want to *survive*.
We want to thrive. We want to up our game.
We want to be happier. We want our lives back —
without all that baggage.

Ten years after the escape, I got married again. I was devastated when it crashed and burned after a few years. No violence or chaos. No fighting, no hurting. Just nothing. Counseling showed me I had gone from chaos and violence in one marriage to withdrawal and silence in the second. ...deep sigh... I finally was able to see the truths   Neither violence or silence are good soil for a deep, committed relationship.

That. Was. It.

I felt so embarrassed. Mortified. How could this have happened again? How utterly ridiculous, I thought. The day he drove away, I decided that this would never happen again. **I decided I would do <u>whatever it took</u> to heal.**

I was so sick of the unhealthy patterns.
Sick of the self-doubt. Sick of the bitterness.
Sick of the heartache. Sick of living angry.
So sick of not trusting myself.

Let's do this. Here is what I've been. Here's what I know. Here is who I am. This is what I offer now in the way of hope and encouragement.

I escaped domestic violence with my three little boys all under the age of seven from a remote volcanic island with a backpack full of pull-ups and snacks (remember, red-eye flight and four layovers with toddlers) and a small cardboard box full of important documents. No luggage.

My family was stunned and surprised. And so very thrilled to get us back alive. They have been amazing. With their help, I picked myself up, became a full-time corporate professional, single mom of three, and started life over. Begin again.

I've been through a long, dark tunnel. I know what it's like to get knocked down. I know what it's like to get back up.

As a helper, you may be helping because you or a loved one suffered trauma. You may simply have a strong sense of justice. Or both. Regardless, you want to help others make their journey more easily.

Sometimes current stress gets to be too much, too heavy. Sometimes current trauma triggers old trauma. Sometimes you forget your boundaries.
Regardless of your past, or why you do what you do, if you tend to carry the stress, worry, fear, or regret, you can start to get physical and emotional

symptoms. These can include chronic fatigue, chronic pain, depression, heart attack, strained relationships, separation, divorce, addiction, suicidal thoughts, cancer, high blood pressure, PTSD, autoimmune diseases.

You see, it's not about what you do. It's not a contest about who has more stress. It's pretty clear that some professions have a higher amount of stress and trauma day-to-day. We're not here to compare. We are here to figure out how to deal with it when is it reality.

Many of us don't deal with trauma every day. And yet many of us have lived through traumatic events.

Depending on how you deal with the stress, it can bleed you dry. If you're a helper, you're the one people call on for help. As a helper, asking for help can feel impossible.

Sometimes you're doing great. Sometimes you're struggling big-time. The struggle is real. Let's get you some tools to mitigate your own stress symptoms. Your own health issues. Your own relationship and parenting issues. Your own self-doubt and fears. It makes sense, doesn't it?

Let's get you less of the issues and baggage and get you more of what you really want.

Spent time in therapy. Took classes. Read some powerful books. Worked through forgiveness issues. Figured some things out. Took accountability for my part of the past. Began to see the puzzle pieces differently than I had before.

I wish I'd known then what I know now.

Would have been easier and I would have healed much more quickly.

We hurt. We learn. We heal. We grow.

I have been a victim. I have been a survivor.
Now I'm a thriver.

Be the thriver now.
Learn now. Heal now. Grow now.
That's right.

I love tools. I love rebuilding. My passion is sharing resilience tools which support and resource others on their journey. Through that season in my life, I decided to do something different. I left my corporate construction management position. I started speaking and training. I have since trained over 10,000 people in live presentations across the country.

This chickadee, who (obviously) had some major relationship baggage in the past, is now married for the first time. Doesn't matter what two sets of divorce papers say. This is the first marriage where I can be myself. What a gorgeous, brilliant blessing.

No one yells. No disrespect. No games.

We talk. We laugh. Yup—we sometimes puzzle over each other's behavior.

We work things out. We compromise. We support each other through the weaknesses. We do our best to give each other space. We talk things out.

We value each other through our strengths. We teach each other. We learn. Then we learn some more.

Diamonds from coal. Beauty from ashes.

Sometimes it's nice to know a bit about who is talking to you, isn't it? (Clock-wise, starting with the spiffy paint respirator.)

PPE (Personal Protective Equipment) is key.
1. I used it for 4 years as a painting contractor.
2. I used it during a K-9 demo exercise I got to be part of. 35# K9 suit. 60# trained canine. Rocket dog. Crazy hard hit.
3. I use it on the track: 35# of gear, helmet and armor.

4. I was honored to train in the main conference room at Andrews Air Force base. This picture was taken at 6:30 am, right before I got to do a 1-day resilience training there. So cool.
Resilience is PPE for LIVING.

When You Value Yourself

When you value yourself, you aren't
guarded. You <u>are</u> still careful.

When you value yourself,
you choose joy.

When you value yourself,
you look peaceful.

When you value yourself,
you stand strong.

When you value yourself,
you sound confident.

When you value yourself,
you feel full.

When you value yourself,
you respond differently.

When you value yourself,
you ask good questions.

When you value yourself,
you set good boundaries.

When you value yourself,
you are resourceful.

When you value yourself,
you can laugh and move on.

When you value yourself,
you forgive yourself and are willing to
consider forgiving others.

When you value yourself,
you love and allow real love.

When you value yourself,
it means you ask for help, seek
answers, and pursue your dreams.

When you value yourself, you live your life.

When you value yourself, you show up in this world differently, don't you? Your stance changes. Your perspective changes. You are treated differently, because you respect yourself differently. If you ask for something and things don't change, you know you have still have options.

When you value yourself, you'll do what takes to get an instant reset so that you can make decisions with clearer thinking and calmer emotions.

If you are reading this right now, it means that you <u>are</u> a heart of courage. You fight. You love. You grow.

You stand up for yourself and then you stand up for others.

You are also very aware that you can only give what you've received.

You know that if you don't take care of yourself, you'll eventually be no good to anyone else.

Yee-ouch.

Yes, that was pretty blunt.

And you know it to be true, don't you?

People talk about self-care. You know how they say it in quotes?

"SELF-CARE." Maybe with a little eye-roll, too.

Why? Because we know we "should" do it. But so often, too often, we don't. Or we may not know how in the middle of life happening.

You can only run at full speed for so long.
You can only hold on by your fingernails for so long.
You can only hold so much, take so much, carry so much, for so long.

You're looking for ways to build your own resilience. You are listening for the next revelation of truth in your life.

You are working to build self-trust and confidence. You are willing to pass it on.

I was teaching this class during a two-day retreat on the west coast recently. During this session, I had an audience member (non-medical, non-emergency responder) ask me, "Isn't this just triage?"

Me: "Great question. Could be. And isn't triage amazing? We get to stop the bleeding and figure out the next step so we don't bleed out. If we cut our hand and need a bandage to stop the bleeding long enough to get to the emergency room, that's a good thing, isn't it?"

The cool thing about these tools is that they stop the bleeding of the stress into other areas of your life.

Get time to collect yourself and think straighter, clearer, and more logically. This slows the burnout cycle.

Get breathing space. Get the time to look at more options. Get the choice to rest instead of to worry. Lose the drama. That's powerful, isn't it?

Imagine for a moment. What if you could learn how to reset your own mindset quickly, easily, and **without having to air your dirty laundry?**

What if changing your thoughts, emotions, and behavior was as easy as using an app on your phone or clicking the remote to change the volume?
Burnout's Kryptonite is like that.

What if you could stop your stress cascade in seconds?

What if you could get yourself balanced out quicker?

What if you could do that without feeling weak?

What if you could do that and not feel like you have to prove yourself all the time?

Get some time and space to get grounded and centered, which means that you have time and energy to make the big decisions that need to be made.

Real life.
Real tools.
Real Resilience.

Why Simple Rocks
(and how it will work for you)

We want to be solid. We want to be stable. We want our lives to be more effective, efficient, and comfortable. We want to have some fun.

To build that in ourselves, we are going to address three resets: Mental, Emotional, Physical.

MENTAL RESET:
You have confident control of your mindset. You are aware what you choose to think about and focus on.

EMOTIONAL RESET:
You are the thermostat, not the thermometer. (Yes, I know. Think about that for a second.) You have confident control of your emotional thermostat.

When you are resilient and confident, you set the tone instead of always being swayed by others and situations around you.

PHYSICAL RESET:
You have confident control of your body. You have good awareness of your physical stance and physiology and how they influence your thoughts, your emotions, and those around you.

Radically Resilient
means having
confident control
of your reset capability.

**Reset   Reset   Get Your
Quicker   Better   Power Back**

How about when you're burned out and don't have any energy left?   How about when you're drowning in hopelessness, you look fried and sound impatient and snarky?

Let's look at Burnout's Kryptonite.

What happens when the bad guy gets kryptonite and delivers it to Superman?   Superman gets weaker, doesn't he? He starts to die. It kills him off. Kills his energy.   Kills his ability to help others.   Kills his ability to do his job, to rescue, to be "Super."

When you think about it, burnout takes it all out of you. You lose energy. You lose your power. You lose your hope. You can't help yourself OR others. Burnout kills your "Super".

What you are doing here is figuring out how to kill burnout. You want to know Burnout's Kryptonite. Let's weaken burnout, take its power, and take its energy out of our lives.

If you think this might be bull, and you've heard it all before, I respect that. I have felt the same way. I mean, how can some simple tools help so much?

Well, is what you're currently doing working? And if not, are you willing to try something different?

Emptiness. Loneliness. Anger. Bitterness. Sadness that won't go away.

Because here's the real deal.

Over 20 years ago, I was on that island we eventually escaped from. I had some tough choices to make.

I was sitting across from the woman who was the first to teach me about boundaries. We were in an intense conversation. Life and death was the topic.

She said, "Ana-Christina. The next time he "restrains" you, it could be with a knife or a gun.

Really—how many times can someone throw you around, knock you down, and wrap their hands around your throat before you get permanently injured or killed?" In the course of the conversation, she said something else that stuck with me.

"Knowledge is power. As you learn about boundaries, you will be able to make different choices." Less than ten days later, my sons and I were escaping. He didn't know we were leaving until we were gone.

New perspective. New choices. New life. Thank God.

Where am I going with this, you ask? Well, I love this woman. I respect this woman. She is a consummate professional. And... in retrospect, I respectfully disagree.

Knowledge isn't power. Knowledge is *potential power*, but not really power in its own right. Knowledge is just knowledge.

Come to think of it... How many people do you know with a certain college degree, but they don't use it or work in it? How many people do you know that "know" how to eat right, but simply don't? Do you know anyone who talks about good relationships and yet is struggling with their own?

APPLIED knowledge is power.
APPLIED knowledge is power.
APPLIED knowledge is power.

Yes, I know I repeated that three times.
It bears repeating. Let's apply it to resilience.

Do you just know the basics of resilience or are you actually <u>doing</u> the basics of resilience? (Knowledge or applied knowledge?)

The basics are the basics because they work. The basics are basics because they are SIMPLE. When you lay resilience as the foundation of your life, it means that you can be more successful, be happier, and be enjoying your life more.

Building resilience without the basics is like trying to build a house without a foundation.

If you can't keep your emotions in check...
If you can't keep your thoughts under control...
If your relationships and health are blowing up...
How do you build the foundation for a great quality life?

Get some SIMPLE tools. APPLY that knowledge. Get some real, usable power in your life.

If you had a choice between simple and complex...

Wouldn't
it
be
better
to
try
simple
first?

Let's get the results with simple tools first. That means that we'll be ready to add other, more complex tools later.

What would
it be like to try
crazy-SIMPLE tools
that help you
GetYourLifeBack?

TOOL 1:
INSTANT MENTAL RESET

Get your thoughts under control FAST.

At the heart of it all, we have an incredibly powerful lens in us which will change how we view the world and what happens to us.

<u>That lens is language</u>.

Our unconscious mind is so powerful. It is always listening to the messages we are using. It's crazy, but our language heavily impacts our perception of reality.

Let's check it out. Right now – look around you and **find at least 5 red things in your environment.**

Yup. Take a second and do it.

Got it? Ok. Now.

Without looking – call out how many YELLOW things are around you right now.

What happened? Did you get all the yellow things?

The fact is that when you focus on red, you see red, right? You don't particularly pay attention to yellow.

Think about it for a moment. What if, for example, instead of simple colors, my lens was dirty and was focused on the jerks around me. Can you imagine if I were to go through my day thinking that everyone else was a total loser? Who am I gonna seem to run into all day long, every day? Jerks and losers. Ug.

It's like having mud on your lenses.

Everything's going to look dark and muddy. Nasty. Negative. Dirty. Awful. Less-than.

Or if you have a bunch of fingerprints all over your lenses, everything looks smudgy, doesn't it? It's especially bad at night when you're tired and your vision is already compromised because of the dark. If you have smudges on your lenses, it makes everything even worse.

If you go around thinking, "The only luck I have is bad luck." What will you see the most? Yup. Nothing but bad luck. You get what you focus on. A negative language lens feeds negative thinking.

I know this sounds familiar. Negative or positive. What you focus on grows. The truth is that you have an absolute POWERHOUSE in your mind.

It's kind of funny, because what we think of as our thinking mind, is our conscious mind. Our brain is taking care of millions of processes that we are never aware of. That is the unconscious mind's job.

Your conscious mind works fast. Super fast, actually. It works at about 40 neural impulses per second. It takes care of the most pressing things going on around you—your lists, your schedule, many of your physical activities.

Your unconscious mind helps take care of what you are thinking about, doing and saying. It also takes care of all of those things you never think about—all of the automatic things that happen to keep you alive, storing all of your memories, keeping millions of body processes rolling along...

Your unconscious mind works at 40... million neural impulses per second.

40 and 40,000,000

You can use the power of both now.

Here's how it works: when you ask a question, it leaves a gap in your thinking. This creates some tension because it is like an empty space that needs to be filled.

The unconscious mind is fast, efficient and it looks for the closest, easiest answer. Once you get an answer, it assumes that it did its job to fill the gap. It can then move on to take care of all those millions of processes happening in your body.

This gap is important because it means that if you ask poor quality questions, you're getting poor quality answers to fill that gap.

Then the unconscious mind moves on. When it moves on in this case, you are left with poor quality answers. That means you have a poor-quality foundation upon which to build your life.

This mental reset tool gives you a different way to think. It sets you up for a stronger foundation.

The chemistry in your body shifts and changes with—believe it or not—your thoughts.

When you get a better grasp on your thoughts—your body can calm down more quickly.

Let's talk about questions. You might be asking them out loud. These are EXTERNAL QUESTIONS.

In the past, I focused on a lot of terrible questions. I did this especially when things were very hard and stressful. No one knew I was thinking that way. These are INTERNAL QUESTIONS.

As you go through this, you will start to become more aware of how many questions you ask each day. Some are external, as speech or writing. Some are internal, as thoughts.

There are three main groups of questions. You'll notice varying degrees of quality.

Crappy-quality questions:
Why am I so... dumb / fat / stupid / slow / poor? Why does this always happen to me? Why can't I ever ___? Why don't they ever ____? Why me?

Better-quality questions:
How might I look at this differently?
How could I learn from this if I chose to?
What can I do? What are they really saying? What else might be happening that I might not know about? What could I learn from this?

Radically Resilient questions:
What other options do I have?
How will I show up? What will I do?
How will I choose to respond to this? What story am I making up about this (that might not be true)? What assumptions am I making? How will I use this in the future? What will I learn from this?

What do these look like, sound like, and feel like?

Let's start with some Crappy Quality Questions and their crappy quality answers. Then we'll move onto Better Quality Q&A. Finally, let's get some Radically Resilient, Burnout-Busting examples!

Crappy Quality Questions

When we ask a crappy question, our unconscious mind (at 40 million neural impulses per second) goes fishing in the crappy quality pool. **Disgusting. Nasty. Putrid. Not a place you want to go fishing.**

Crappy quality questions are blame-focused, whiny, think the worst, play victim/martyr, and generally have a crappy tone.

Mechanics of the question: Typically starts with Why and then focuses on who's to blame and what's wrong.

Example 1: I made a mistake.
Example 2: I am overweight.
Example 3: They do something that annoys me.

Crappy Quality Q&A: mistake
Q: Why am I so stupid?
A: Well—because I don't apply yourself. Because I didn't finish school. Because I am lazy.

Crappy Quality Q&A: weight
Q: Why can't I lose weight?"
A: Because I don't have good self-discipline. I never exercise enough. Because I eat like crap. I've tried everything and nothing works. [Notice the victim stance?]

Crappy Quality Q&A: something that annoys me
Q: Why doesn't s/he ever change?
A: Because s/he doesn't care. Because they simply can't be bothered. Because they don't love or respect me enough to change. Because they just want to piss me off. (So often the crap answer.)

This probably already sounds familiar. Our brain starts to fill in the blanks after it goes to the crappy quality pool for answers. Nasty, unhelpful answers.

You get to choose. Is this a place where you want to spend your time, energy, thoughts, emotional energy and life?

What might
happen
if you
started fishing
in a different
thought pool?

Better Quality Questions

When you use Better Quality Questions, you take more accountability. You don't blame, are solution-focused, look for options, get curious, and generally chill out. Your unconscious uses its 40,000,000 to go fishing in a better quality pool.

Mechanics of the Question: Starts with How or What. Focuses on potential options, choices, solutions. Assumes control over yourself instead of trying to control others.

Example 1: I made a mistake.
Example 2: I am overweight.
Example 3: They do something that annoys me.

Better Quality Q&A: mistake
Q: What am I good at?
What could I do to get more training / experience?
How could I get more information on this?
What could I try next time?
A: I am good at figuring things out. I could get a mentor. I could Google or YouTube it. I could think before I act / speak. I could try slowing down.

Better Quality Q&A: weight
Q: What small step could I take toward losing weight and gaining muscle? How will I make this time different? What can I do to get some support? What can I do to eat differently that actually works with my schedule?
A: [How are your answers different now?]

<u>Better Quality Q&A: something that annoys me.</u>
Q: What could I do differently to give her/him a kind reminder?   How might I look at the situation differently?   What's <u>really</u> important to me—and, is this worth the battle?   How could I put humor into this?
A: [How does this change your answers?]

Your unconscious mind starts to fill in the blanks after it goes to the better quality pool for answers. Your answers have started shifting already, haven't they?

What could I … ?
What might I … ?
What would I do if … ?
How else could I … ?
How else can I … ?

You may not be sure how to do this yet, but are you interested in knowing how to fish in an even better pool?

The more you practice, the more aware you become.

What I believe,
I empower.

When I ask better questions
I get better answers.

When I use my language
to reflect my beliefs
in a more positive direction,
it means that I build a stronger
foundation for my life.

Radically Resilient Questions

* **Focus on the solution.**
* **Help you get your power back.**
* **Frame the question positively.**
* **Create a can-do mindset.**
* **Take full accountability for what YOU can control. Are focused on how YOU are going to show up, regardless of the circumstances.**

When you choose this lens, it will change your perspective.

It effectively clears and cleans the crap and dirt off. A lot nicer pool to fish in, isn't it?

Example 1: I made a mistake.
Example 2: I am overweight.
Example 3: They do something that annoys me.

Radically Resilient: mistake
Q: How will I figure this out?
What will I do differently next time?
How will I apply this and change things up?
What resources do I have available to me?
How will I apologize sincerely?
What other options do I have? What did I learn?

Radically Resilient: weight
Q: What will I put in place to make this plan work?
How will I get support for my new food choices?
What else will I try? Who do I know that has made it work? What did they do?

Radically Resilient: something that annoys me.
Q: What is <u>really</u> important here?
How will I show that <u>they</u> are more important than their behavior? How will I choose to behave, even if they don't change?

Answers: [How are your answers drastically different now?]

When you ask a better question, is means that you get a better answer.

As you ask better questions, your lens stays cleaner When you ask a better question, your resilience foundation gets stronger.

I'm not thinking those examples were deep or earth-shattering.   I can appreciate that because they seem trivial…. AND…

How often has a trivial thing been the straw that broke your back?

How often has the smallest thing blown up into a full-blown argument that ruined your night / day / week / month / relationship?

Trivial, small things can add up if you let them, don't they?

Asking a better question means you have more control.

1. More control over how you look: Asking a better question means knowing you have full, 100% control of how you show up. You stand tall. You look confident.

2. More control over how you sound: Asking a better question means you get to trade in the piss, moan and whine for a confident tone. You will sound more congruent once you think about, and act upon, your answers.

3. More control over how you feel: Asking a better question means you get to trade tired, put-upon, roll-your-eyes-frustration for confident resilience. You feel better, you feel more congruent, you can be more present and boundaried.

Look, sound, and be more confident.
Anytime.
Anywhere.
With anyone.

If you've gotten this far, and you are still reading, it means you are dedicated to change and growth.

It means that you are resourceful and wanting more from life. Now you can do this even better!

P.S. Fly higher.
See page 125 for The Great Big Beautiful List of Radically Resilient Questions.
Enjoy.

76   Burnout's Kryptonite

TOOL 2:
INSTANT EMOTIONAL RESET

78   Burnout's Kryptonite

Get confident control of your emotions now.

Do you ever have trouble with your emotions? Yelling, anger, tears, venting, the silent treatment.

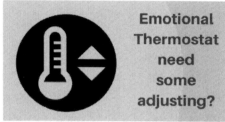

Emotional Thermostat need some adjusting?

At one time or another, you may notice that one second, you're ok, and the next you melt down, shut down, or explode. Or maybe you stuff your emotions and then they build up and threaten to drown you.

This tool works because it's your neuro-physiology.

Let's do some brain science! The amygdala is a small, almond-shaped organ in the center of the brain. **It's built to react to life or death situations.** It is responsible for fight / flight / freeze reactions. If something can potentially kill you, the amygdala is paying attention.

The amygdala doesn't have a calendar. It doesn't know if it is past, present or future right now. Here is what it DOES know. It is responsible for holding onto memories, especially he ones with high negative emotion or trauma. That way, it can warn you if something like this ever happened before so that you can avoid it now.

It's part of our survival instinct. It's how we were built. This is where it gets very cool. Unfortunately, this is also where the trouble starts. Let's check it out.

The reason your amygdala reacts this way is **because it needs to react instantaneously if danger is present.** It gets signals from your eyes, ears, touch, smell and taste through your brain stem.

It checks its catalog of memories to see if anything like this present situation has happened before. If it was dangerous in the past, the body instantly goes into threat readiness mode. Because of this, if an old trigger gets pressed, it can feel like the past experience is happening right now.

Let's test this. Can you remember something that happened in the past that **angered you?**

Try to think of a specific instance at least ten years ago that was very upsetting

Imagine the details: what you were seeing, what you were hearing, what you were feeling. Where were you, who was around, what was your reaction? How did you feel? Were you in potential danger of any sort? What were you afraid of? Was it confusing? Were people freaking out? Were you freaking out? Did you go numb?

If I asked you to think about it for a few minutes, focus on the details, run through the blow-by-blow, what would start happening? If I had you tell me all about it, visualize every detail and every horrible feeling coursing through your body—what might happen? If you focused on it, could you still get upset about it?

Almost everyone has a memory like this. When I ask, people often say, "Yes—I can feel myself getting upset again." They report an agitated feeling, their hackles go up, their heart beats faster and / or their breathing changes. They've begun to feel upset again **even though it happened over ten years ago.**

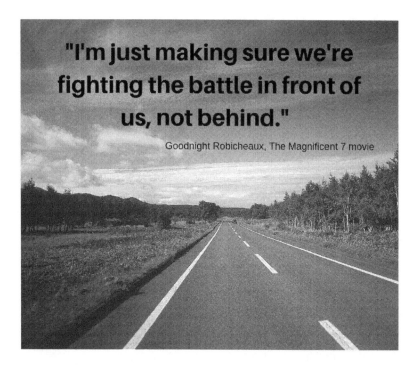

"I'm just making sure we're fighting the battle in front of us, not behind."

Goodnight Robicheaux, The Magnificent 7 movie

That is mainly due to an amygdala response. It starts to send off signals to get you ready to protect yourself in the present even though the event that holds the traumatic memory happened years ago.

When the amygdala detects a potential threat, it goes on high-alert. The brain gets and sends threat signals, you dump adrenaline, testosterone, cortisol and multiple other neurotransmitters and hormones to get you ready for fight / flight / freeze.

The problem, of course, is staying in that hypervigilant mode. Regardless of your work, your job, your family life, if you're constantly stressed, your body tends to go into hypervigilance.

I had a client who had suffered a series of tragic accidents with her children, one after another. Life-threatening, multiple surgeries which were incredibly painful for the children, and horrible for the parents to watch. Add sleepless nights, expensive medical bills, and time intensive care-giving. Over a period of years, this creates unbelievable stress, hypervigilance, and burn out.

Hypervigilance is linked to high cortisol & high epinephrine levels. High cortisol has been increasingly linked to the following health concerns: (here's the fine print – and this is only a partial list.)
Weight gain (especially around mid-section), sleep problems, fertility issues, hormone imbalance, muscle tension, breathing issues, muscle aches and

pains, adrenal fatigue, mood swings, puffy face, flushed skin, acne, lowered immunity, high blood pressure, increased anxiety, increased urination, changes in libido, irregular period, excessive thirst, higher risk for bone fractures and osteoporosis.

You recognize any of those in yourself?

Hypervigilance can happen when thinking about past negative events, past dangerous situations, past trauma. It can spike with current anxiety-producing situations in your life. It can happen when you imagine a potential conflict or tough conversation that you need to have and you don't expect it to go well. Hypervigilance can try to take over with anything that raises fear and anxiety levels. (Like bills, health concerns, family conflict, or fights with your significant other.)

If the amygdala gets stuck in the emotion, whether or not it's life or death right now, it fires off your acute stress response. If it happens often, the amygdala can get "hot" and stays hypervigilant. Over time, this can elevate your cortisol, which acts like poison to your body

How do we begin to calm down when we feel the anxiety or fear rising up?

This tool effectively short-circuits the threat-messages coming from the brain stem and cuts off the anxious instincts of the amygdala. What's this cool tool?

Active Appreciation.
Intentional gratitude.
Out-loud-thanks.

It's the way your brain is built.

When you are **actively** thinking of things to be thankful for, it stops the amygdala from operating at the wrong time for the wrong reasons. Therefore, it halts the escalation of the acute threat response.

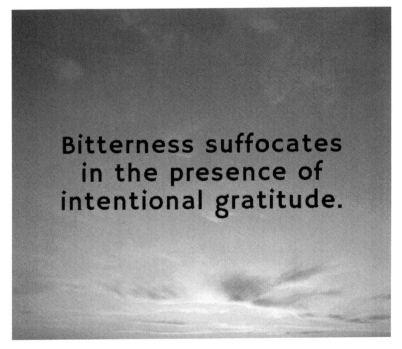

Bitterness suffocates in the presence of intentional gratitude.

Physiologically, the state of active appreciation short-circuits the amygdala.

BIG IMPORTANT TRUTH: The threat system and the thankful systems cannot fire simultaneously.

That means that when we make the choice to be thankful, grateful, praising, or appreciative, we quite literally cannot be afraid at the same exact moment.

You may already know this, down deep. If you continue to focus on the negative in the situation, then the negative-emotion fire will start again. For example, if you throw negative thought-fuel on it, your fear will fire up and gain strength. You get to choose whether or not to throw that negative fuel.

This might also seem familiar. Active appreciation is Kryptonite to fear. Fear must die in the presence of active gratitude. Brilliant, isn't it?

It means that when you choose to focus on positive thought-fuel, the fear has to leave. The secret is to use the tools as often as necessary to combat the acute fear response. <u>Then you can decide what to do next</u>.

You can start by being thankful, out loud, for things around you that are good. You can also make a list of things you're thankful for, ahead of time and keep it handy. Use as often as needed. Might be a dozen times a day.

Ah, but what happens when life is tough and you can't seem to come up with good things right now? How about when life feels crushing?

Active Appreciation Script for tough times. (Lord knows I need something simple when things are crashing down.)

To be clear, I am not saying to be thankful for the trauma or the horrible thing that is happening or just happened. Let that sink in. Instead, I am saying to find a way to be thankful in spite of the circumstances. You get to be creative and flexible because you want this emotional reset. You find a way, make a way, imagine a way to be thankful even if, even though, or even when something ugly happened.

You are not denying the horrible thing, so you go ahead and call it out. It is finding a way to be thankful for something in the midst of the pain and injustice. In spite of it. Regardless of the fact that it happened. You get to choose.

Active Appreciation Script
for tough times:

"I am thankful / grateful / appreciative

+

even if / even though / even when

+

_____ ."

(fill in the blank with the bad or painful thing that is happening.)

Examples:

* I am thankful + even if + I don't understand why that happened.
* I am grateful + even though + I have no idea how I'm going to pay that bill.
* I am thankful + even when + I'm hurting and sad.
* I appreciate my job even when it's tough.
* I choose to be grateful even when they didn't do it the way I wanted.
* I choose to be thankful for what I have even if I am not sure what the next step is.

What you focus on grows. When you focus on the appreciation, your amygdala stops firing like crazy. Your stress-response will de-escalate. One simple and quick reset is the act of thanking.

Q&A:

Q: Do I have to do this out loud?

A: No, and it does help especially at first. Start by saying it out loud, by yourself, for two minutes. Many of my clients comment that it helps them focus to thank out loud or in writing.

Q: Do I have to thank someone?

A: No. It's for you and reducing your anxiety. You can imagine thanking someone if that is helpful. And—thanking someone out loud can help as well.

Q: What happens if I feel afraid or upset again when I stop being appreciative?

A: **What you focus on, grows**.

If you start to focus on the negative or upsetting thoughts again, your focus goes there and you will likely feel your threat response go up again. The cool thing is that you have control over this. You get to choose. You get to work the tool. Use as often as necessary. During tough times, you'll be doing a lot of thanking. Your emotions will settle within minutes during the active appreciation you're practicing.

Your thoughts calm, and because of this, your emotions will stabilize more quickly.

Decide where you are going to place your focus.

Don't give up if it doesn't work right away. Use the tools. Practice, grab hold, and use them when you need them.

Keep going. Keep going. Keep going.
You can so do this.

Asking Radically Resilient questions, active appreciation, and the third tool will act as a powerful, simple, quick arsenal to combat fear, worry, and burnout.

You've gotten this far.

It means change and growth will be easier than ever before.

That's right.

90   Burnout's Kryptonite

I am aware.
I am thankful.
I receive this moment's gift.

Even when it's dark, I will seek the Light.
Even when it's silent, I will seek Hope.
Even when it's cold, I will seek the Warmth.
Because...

When I look up, it means I am still in the fight.
When I listen, it means I am willing to grow.
When I feel my heartbeat, it means I am ready to try.

I am aware.
I am thankful.
I receive this moment's gift.

TOOL 3:
INSTANT PHYSICAL RESET

Get calmer in seconds.

Can you remember a time when:
1) you felt your stress spike when it **wasn't** life or death?
2) fear hit you hard and there wasn't any apparent reason for it?
3) you got red-hot angry over a tiny small thing?

Examples?
A huge bill you don't know how you're going to pay.
An old, bad memory hits you unexpectedly.
Fight with your loved one.
Nasty-gram from a friend.
Seems like there's no way out.
Heated misunderstanding.
You can't problem-solve like you need to.
You feel cornered.
A loved one is in big trouble and you can't help.
Unjust reprimand from your boss.
Humiliation in front of your peers.
Crappy interaction with a patient / client?
Fill in your blank _____

If you can picture a frog or a box, you can reduce stress in seconds.

Physically, when you have a stress response, you tend to breathe faster and more shallowly. These tools reverse that.

Use it BEFORE, DURING, AFTER.
This next tool will prepare you for the situation, help you during the situation, and reset you quicker after the situation. Or the bad day. Or an expected confrontation. Or a meeting or interview or appointment you're stressed about.

Meet your nervous systems. Both of them.

Parasympathetic nervous system = REST / DIGEST.
This controls your rest and digest response. It controls homeostasis. Homeostasis is the state of balance in your body, your body at rest, and your digestion processes. The deep, slow breathing that we do when in deep sleep can trigger this system. This system can also be triggered by **intentional, deliberate, deep breathing**. That means that you can control it!

Sympathetic nervous system = THREAT.
This system controls your threat response. It controls your body's reactions to a perceived threat and is responsible for the **fight/flight/freeze** stress response. Shallow breathing is a result of using this system. The system can also be triggered by fast, shallow breathing. That means we have control over it when we're aware of it.

This next tool can be done in so many ways. We are going to cover two ways right now. The next two breathing tools will bring you back into rest and digest, your parasympathetic nervous system. Either tool will pull you out of fight/flight/freeze threat-response escalation.

These tools will bring you back into balance. Lower heart rate, slower breathing, lower blood pressure, calmer emotions, and clearer thoughts.

We don't have direct control over many systems in our bodies—digestion, heartbeat, tastebuds, internal organs, neurotransmitter secretion, perspiration, etc.

When you think about it, breathing is one of the only internal systems in our body that we can easily control.

It's free. It's quick. Easy. Anytime. Anywhere. With anyone.

AND—it has a significant effect on the chemical, hormonal, and neurotransmitter cascades that affect all these other systems!

Belly Breathing.
Box Breathing.

Navy Seals use it.

Marines use it.

Firefighters are being trained to use it.

You can use it.

We will practice the two techniques now. You can do them one at a time or do them together.

Belly Breathing—

Marine Corps professionals focus on belly breathing (or diaphragmatic breathing.) Super-crazy simple.

Belly Breathing: Place your hands over your heart to start. Partly to be aware of your heart, and mostly to feel your chest. If your chest heaves and your shoulders are going up... then you're not breathing from your belly.

Keep your chest as still as possible, keep your shoulders stable, and breathe by pushing your belly out for the inhale and pulling your abs in for the exhale. The belly is acting like a pump to bring air in and out. This uses the whole set of lungs instead of only the top of the lungs.

PRACTICE:
Chest = stays still.
Shoulders = stay down and relaxed.

Put your hands flat on your belly and feel it going in and out. This can be easier if you practice lying on your back.

BREATHE IN = BELLY OUT.
Your abs are pushing out, so they create suction on the diaphragm and draw in air to expand the lungs.

BREATHE OUT = BELLY IN.
As you exhale, pull belly in.
Breathe out as your tighten up your belly.
It squeezes your diaphragm up and pushes air out of your lungs.

Take ten deep, rich, life-giving belly breaths.

Box or Square Breathing—

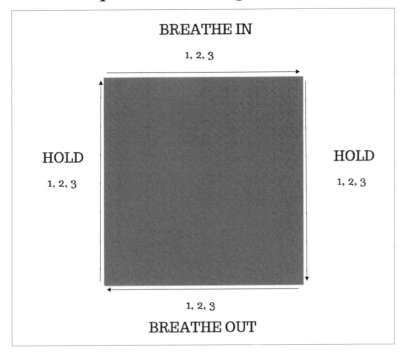

Navy Seals focus on the Box or Square breathing technique – also called Combat Breathing.

Box Breathing: Breathe through the full count of three.

Breathe in the for count of 3:   1,2,3.
Hold breath for count of 3:   1,2,3.
Breathe out for the count of 3:   1,2,3.
Hold breath for count of 3:   1,2,3.

PRACTICE:

Breathe along with the instructions as you are tracing the box on the left page with your index finger. Do that at least three times.

Now, imagine the box in front of you instead. Do the exercise in the air, tracing the imaginary box with your index finger. Three times.

Finally, put your arms down and do the whole exercise, imagining the box in front of you, but not tracing it. Do this three times.

It works because that is how you are built.

Start with the Belly. Practice several times a day. Slow your count.

Practice the Box. Several times a day. Slow your count as you practice.

Bonus: Do it stealth. Practice your box while doing something else. Practice your Belly while in a conversation. Notice what happens in your body.

Imagine what will happen when you practice <u>before</u> you get into that super-frustrating situation.

Imagine what will happen when you practice before you get stressed out.

Imagine how your relationships will change up when you practice before you get into a fight or "heated discussion." And then USE IT DURING the discussion.

Imagine how your relationships will shift as you begin to use this even when you are in the middle of judging, getting ticked, snarky, or upset. Those emotions will start to melt away when you breathe intentionally.

Imagine how you will show up differently when you begin to feel those old fears, anxieties and worries. You now have a tool that you can apply to get an instant reset, instead.

The fact is that we deal with fear sometimes.
Unfortunately, fear, anxiety and worry don't just shrivel up, die and go away forever. Even when you process and deal with the old baggage, new stuff comes up.

Because these tools are based on how the brain works, it means that they have to work, <u>when you use them</u>.

Now you can do this even better. Calm. Fast. Now.

Launch Into Your Life

(Photo disclaimer. This picture was a photo of my practice ON THE RUNWAY before we took off. I am three feet above the ground. No 130 mph prop-driven air blasting my face. No 12,000 foot altitude. No clouds next to me. Just wanted to clarify why I'm smiling and why my skin isn't trying to peel off my cheekbones like in the picture at the end of the chapter...)

I'd never been "out the door." Skydiver term. It means I'd never done a tandem jump (instructor on your back), much less solo.

I kid you not—I used these tools to calm down after an almost-meltdown at 12,500 feet above the earth.

I took an eight-hour class to prepare to skydive for the first time. In fact, I was taken aback when we learned that once we jump out of the plane, we are, according to the FAA, piloting a single wing aircraft...) (What in the world are they doing allowing me to fly this thing after only eight hours of training?) (What?!) (Sheesh.) (No pressure...)

Ah, but I digress. Here we are. Right here...talking about jumping out of a perfectly good aircraft.

The thing about skydiving? That first step's a doozie.

In the picture you just saw, I was asked to practice my exit as I stepped into the plane. Something unexpected happened to me during that practice.

We were on the runway and there was no prop-driven wind pressing me into the plane (which is what happens when you go to make your exit and jump). Because of that, I felt like I was falling out of the plane. It didn't matter that there was a staircase right there, I was three feet off the ground, and my instructor was right next to me. I don't know what happened, but panic started.

Even though we were going **zero mph,** panic hit me hard and fast. It came without any warning at all. My heart was racing before I ever sat down with my super-cool rental helmet (haha) and 35-pound parachute on my back, squished between two other jumpers.

Aside: This is similar to what can happen when you don't have resilience dialed into your life. The big scary awful things happen and you have no more room on your plate. You have no more resources when you're running dry. You have no more to give when you're running on empty, do you? And sometimes – it's the small tiny thing, or a very unexpected thing that tips you over. Sometimes it's a painful event. Sometimes it's a small thing or comment you've dealt with dozens of times that hits you wrong. Tips you over the edge. Either way, it throws you and it feels impossible to bounce back.

As I kept focusing on that huge hole in the side of the plane, things went sideways. **Way sideways.**

I thought about all the things they said could go wrong. Like not finding the airport. Like running into a building. Like landing in a lake. Like the chute not opening. And then the secondary chute not opening. CRAP. (Crappy quality thoughts.) Then I wondered if I would remember all the safety procedures. Would I be able to land ok? THEN full-blown panic punched me in the gut.

I decided that <u>my butt was not leaving that seat</u> until I'd ridden that plane down to the ground like any self-respecting, logical, normal, have-my-priorities-straight human being.

It didn't matter that I'd just finished taking a comprehensive eight-hour class.

It didn't matter that the jump was a life-long dream.

Didn't matter that my whole family knew what I was doing that day.

It didn't matter that my best friend and bond, my then-fiancé-now-husband, Wilson, had purchased the jump for me for my 50th birthday.

It didn't matter that I was going to waste over $400.

I. DID. NOT. CARE.

Ton of bricks on my chest. My heart pounding out through the bricks. Couldn't think. Couldn't reason. Nothing. Nada. NOHOW. Nothing mattered except the huge fear and anxiety battering my senses. My heart was racing. I was panicking.

I was jumping with two instructors by my side, but sheesh. I'd be by myself once I pulled the chute.

Well, that thought didn't help at all when the adrenaline was dumping into my brain and body.

I thought about all the reasons not to jump.

Dozens and dozens of reasons not to jump. Then the expletives inside my head. Crap. *&%$#! Crap. Cr

(Ok. To be fair. Those weren't *exactly* the words. I do believe I had other, way more colorful ones going. Yup.)

The thing that got me to snap out of it?

I asked myself (and I was pretty stern about it, too): **"ANA-CHRISTINA—WHAT DO YOU TEACH?"**

Aside: The only time I'd <u>ever felt this degree of panic</u> was the three critical hours when I was escaping from that tiny Alaskan island with my three little boys that day over 20 years ago. Our lives were on the line and the panic was almost paralyzing. Fast forward to this plane...the one I was supposed to jump out of.

So I thought—What do I teach? Seals use it. Marines use it. I'm gonna try.

I tried to Belly-Box breathe. It didn't work right away. Let me tell you why.

At first, I couldn't do the Box because my brain didn't work enough to do the Box. Too many numbers (chuckle). Yes, really. Too many numbers.

So I started with the Belly.

Once I got the Belly under control, I went to the Box. It seemed like an eternity before I felt better (was probably 30-45 seconds.) Then I felt better and stopped breathing. Oops. Don't do that.

Started looking at that big gaping door covered with plexiglass, imagining... not good things.

What if I forget my safety protocols?
What if the chute doesn't open?
What if the reserve gets tangled?
(Recognize the crappy quality questions? They are all negative.)

CrapandcrapandcrapandwhydidIeversignupforthis?

I freaked out and felt the panic rise again.
(It stopped working because I focused on the bad stuff and threw negative thought-fuel on the fear. On cue, it fired right up!)

So I started again.
Stayed with it.
Focused on the Belly.
THEN focused on the Box.
Then went all out and did them together.

Wait for it. Wait for it...

Aaaaaaaaaand 1...2...3...

Whew.

I could think again.

And as soon as I could (amygdala disrupted), I started being thankful. I was thanking for everything I could think of. Focused on that for a bit. Then I started being able to ask better questions.

I thought about my reason to jump.

Q: What am I doing here? What do I truly want?

A: To expand my comfort zone.

To know that I pushed past a tough spot.

To try something tough I'd never tried before.

To know that I can control the fear **instead** of letting it control me. Super important.

It was important for me to do it.
Not for anyone else.
For <u>me</u>.

So – I chose to try the things I'd practiced because I wanted a certain result.

Within approximately two minutes, I had control again and could answer my instructor again (we were knee to knee in the tiny plane). I continued being thankful and grateful with my active appreciation.

These techniques worked to the point that I had zero fear launching myself out over northern Colorado at 12,500 feet at about 130 mph.

Remarkable. A rush, to be sure, but more than that, an affirmation of pressing into, through and out of the fear and into Peace. Imagine.

Floating in the sheer hugeness of the sky.

Looking around and seeing the curvature of the earth on the horizon.

Totally silent except for the rippling of the canopy above and the crisp, clear air against my face.

Brilliant. Truly brilliant.

LIVE.
YOUR.
LIFE.

That was quite a day.

When we press into the fear, when we work the process, when we come out the other side with a learning… then we've won the battle, haven't we?

If you read this little book, you are a helper. I am thankful for your skill, your competence, your compassion, and your dedication. I appreciate what you do, day after day.

I don't know your story. I don't know how you got here or what you're dealing with. I hear stories. Lots and lots of stories from professionals across the U.S. I can only imagine the stuff you've been through.

You. You are making it through. You are pressing into life.

I know that the people you help may be in crisis when you are helping them. They are hurting, upset, angry or messed up. Life can be painful, shocking, and sad.

I also get that you don't get near enough thank-yous. **I thank you.**

Next step: Pick one tool from this book (only one for now) and try it for seven days. If you miss a day, keep going. Notice the shifts that are happening as you do this. Which tool are you going to focus on for the next seven days?

These tools will give you strength, little by little, to do the things you know you need to do.

Getting your head on straight - doing a bit of triage regularly - means that you will have more energy, clearer thinking, and higher confidence.

These tools will help you make the changes you know you need to make.

GetYourLifeBack.

I'd love to know how it's working for you.
    - *ANA-CHRISTINA* www.toolsofhope.com

The Wind Beneath Your Wings

It's about fierce freedom and relentless hope.
Harness your power.

HARNESS YOUR POWER
Discover your plan. Uncover your purpose.
Live the life you were created to live.

HARNESS YOUR POWER
See the reality. See the opportunity.
Build your new reality.

HARNESS YOUR POWER
People do this. You can do this.
You are flexible. You are open. You are asking.
You realize you have more resources than ever before.

HARNESS YOUR POWER
Learn to love the process. Choose. Enjoy the small things.
Learn to love seeking the path.

HARNESS YOUR POWER
Come to the battle. Fight for your own healing.
Press into that place of peace that
soothes your mind, heart, and soul.

We want that. Sometimes, it can seem so hard. Hopelessness and discouragement aren't sexy topics. Not juicy. Not popular. Not good.

I get it. I've been hopeless and discouraged. My sons and I started our lives over many years ago. I let the pain last for far too long after we got out. It can be frustrating, exhausting, debilitating.

And real. Often, we don't know how to deal with other people's emotions, much less our own. So we don't go there. We mask it.

* With busyness.
* With a drink. And then another…
* With a smile and, "I'm good – how are you?" even though you feel like you're dying inside.
* With stuffing it down and out of sight.
* With "Everything is awesome and great" posts on social media while our lives are falling apart behind closed doors. As one of my mentors said, "On social media, we look at everyone else's highlight reel and compare it to our blooper reel."

It's not cool or sexy to talk about the deep dark hole that haunts us even though we look, sound, and seem successful. We value holding it all together versus BEING ALL TOGETHER.

Being all together means being whole and honest. With ourselves first, then the world.

It means being congruent in your thoughts, feelings, and actions. Congruence means facing the tough so that you can move on with your mind, heart, body, soul and spirit all pulling in the same direction.

Knowing what you truly want is intimately connected to knowing who you are.

To get there, you get to ask yourself some powerful questions.

What is important to me?

What do I believe in, when all else fails?

Who do I count on?

Who do I listen to?

Who do I look to?

What do I stand on?

What do I do that gives me LIFE?

Taking time and space to get crystal clear on your values, what you want out of your life, and what is most important to you is a first step.

Knowing who you are and what you want? Now THAT'S exciting. Energizing. Thrilling.

<u>Steps to get your wings</u>:
1. Choose to be willing.
2. Choose to let go what no longer serves.
3. Choose to be aware of the learnings.
4. Choose to embrace the joy.

You were built for such a time as this.

You are unique. There has never been anyone like you. You have a remarkable and special set of gifts, talents and experiences that no one else can bring to bear.

You have hurt. You have suffered. It's time to heal. Step by step, moment by moment. People do this. It's _your_ time to heal.

You are meant to shine light into the darkness.
I call you into your true self.
I call you into love, joy, peace, patience.
Powerful heart, I call you into the place which brings hope.

BELOVED

Beloved. Beautiful. Powerful.
Brilliant heart and soul.

You were built to have peace in a year of drought and always bear fruit.

You were built to receive so you can give.

You were built as a stream of living water for those you love. For those you serve.

You were built for joy. You were built for love.
You were built for peace. You were built for patience.

No matter what has gone before, you can begin again.

You are meant to listen. You are meant to create.
You are meant to love. You are meant to lead.

You are meant to risk.
You are meant to be safe and protected.

You are meant to focus. You are meant to play.

You are meant to be curious. You are meant to trust.

You live thankful, aware, grounded.

You are meant to uncover who you are.
There is a plan for your life. There is a purpose for you.

Find your wings, my dear. Use your wings, beloved.

It's time to FLY.

Flying Higher

The Great Big Beautiful List of Radically Resilient Questions

Think Clearer

Think Faster

Rock Your Confidence

As you consider this, you'll become much more aware of your language patterns. It builds on what you've learned and takes it to a whole new level.

1) Start to notice your thought and language patterns in a whole new way.

2) Start to change the structure of your questions which means that you will begin to impact the quality of your life.

3) Start to use The Great Big Beautiful List of Radically Resilient Questions for quick mental resets.

Thought Starter:

The quality of your question determines the quality of your answer. In order to get an instant mental reset… you can ask a better quality question.

Thoughts spinning out of control?

Anger getting the best of you?

Can't think positively no matter how much you try?

These questions help when your thoughts are tangled or out of control.

These questions will help you combat fear, confusion, anger, sadness.

These questions will help…

* When things go wrong.

* When things just went wrong… again.

* When you have no idea how to stay positive.

* When you are sad and feeling discouraged.

* When you want to understand, but can't. Life can seem so unfair.

* When you don't know what to do.

* When you can't get those visuals / sounds / feelings out of your head.

* When you want something different.

* When you want to brainstorm like a rockstar.

* When you want to move forward.

QUICK REVIEW:

"Crappy" or Poor Quality Questions…
Tear down / Are negative / Have no action.

What are the go-to poor quality questions that you have asked in the past? (In thoughts or words?)

Unfortunately, these questions go fishing in the "crappy" quality pool .

Asking poor quality questions leads to nothing but poor quality answers, victim-thinking, and a stuck life.

Starter Word	Negative Structure	Who	Blaming
Why	can't	she / he / they	ever...
Why	doesn't	she/he	ever..
Why	am	I	so...

Examples:
Why am I so… dumb / stupid / slow / fat / clumsy?
Why can't I ever do this?
Why do things always go wrong for me?
Why can't she ever ___?
Why doesn't he ever ____?
Why won't they ever _____?
Why am I never chosen?
Why me? Why? Why? Whine. Whine. Whine.

QUICK REVIEW:

Better Quality Questions…
Build up / Take ownership / Are positive / Take some action.

Starter	Soft Verb	Who	Positive Action
How / What	can	I / we	do / think / imagine…
How / What	could	I / we	create / learn / develop / adjust…
How / What	might	I / we	shift / change / grow…
How / What	would	I / we	look / perceive / listen / feel / sense…

Examples:

How might I look at this differently?
How could I learn from this if I chose to?
What might I think differently?
What can I learn / do / say?
How could I respond in a healthier way?
What could I do to change my perspective?
How else could I look at this?
What could I learn from this?

QUICK REVIEW:

Radically Resilient Questions…

Build up / Develop new possibilities / Take responsibility / Open up choice / Are positive / Invite action / Create power and strength thinking.

Start	Strong Verb	Who	Choice	Positive action
How / What	will / shall	I / we		think / imagine / shift / practice / work on / commit… ?
How / What	am	I	willing to	do / create / learn / develop / make / look / perceive / feel / sense…?
How / What	are	we	going to	celebrate / delight / learn / change…?
How / What	am/are	I / we	choosing to	show / demonstrate / love / appreciate / forgive…

The Great Big Beautiful List
of Radically Resilient Questions:

1. How WILL I choose to answer / act / communicate?

2. What WILL I choose to think / feel?

3. What DO I want to be in this moment?

4. How AM I going to show up?

5. How will I choose to see this differently?

6. What will I choose to learn from this?

7. How am I going to respond?

8. What are my options?

9. How can I adjust to this situation?

10. What else could I consider?

11. What ELSE could I do?

12. What other options are there?

13. What other options do I have?

14. What is another choice?

15. What will I decide to do THIS time?

16. What will I decide to do NOW?

17. What will I decide to do next time?

18. How am I going to change this going forward?

19. How can I serve and add value?

20. What will make the biggest difference right now?

21. What assumptions am I making?

22. How am I willing to acknowledge the learning in the midst of this?

23. How else could I be thinking about this?

24. What else might be happening that I have no clue about?

25. What are three potential ways to fix this?

26. What does this mean for this relationship?

27. How could I show up differently and break the negative pattern?

28. How shall I be more curious next time?

29. What will I put into place so that this doesn't happen again?

30. What am I going to commit to that will change the outcome?

31. What does this mean?

32. What is the advantage for me in this?

33. How does this change me?

34. What am I missing? What should I be seeing?

35. What do I need to hear here?

36. What stance do I choose to take?

37. How will I stop complaining and start repairing?

38. How will I control my OWN attitude?

39. How will I choose to stop the gossip and start building up?

40. What could we do together?

41. How could I cooperate differently?

42. What shall I try instead?

43. How would I rather do it?

44. What would I prefer instead?

45. Even now, how do I keep my head on straight?

46. What is this telling me about things I want to change about myself?

47. What would I have to believe in order to feel better about this?

48. What is my part in this?

49. What am I being invited to let go of?

50. What is the learning here?

51. How can I hold onto the learning and let go of the negative emotions?

52. What is a super creative way that I could go about solving this?

53. How could we team up on this instead of fighting?

54. What is TRULY important here and how can I show that?

55. How do I "pick my battles" on this one?

56. What is going on behind the scenes?

57. How am I blowing this out of proportion?

58. What baggage is this bringing up? (If I'm honest, I may be over-reacting on this.)

59. What judgements am I making that are making this whole thing worse?

60. What am I going to choose to do with those judgements?

61. How am I going to cut myself some slack on this instead of beating myself up?

62. How could we come together as a team on this?

63. How shall I love them regardless?

64. How will I focus on loving myself?

65. What will I do to ensure that I am in the best possible place to be making this decision?

66. How will I make sure I am in the right frame of mind to follow through?

And the last one on **The Great Big Beautiful List of Radically Resilient Questions?**

Not sure if this every happens to you, but when I am struggling, I can't remember a whole list of questions. So my "go-to" is the LEARNING.

IT'S ALL ABOUT THE LEARNING, isn't it?

I know you're curious. What is one of the most powerful questions, regardless of the situation?

67. What is the positive learning?

At it's simplest, pick a variation on **learning**.

What am I **learning**? What is the **learning**?
What is there to **learn** from this, that, if I **learn** it, I can let go the negative emotions that have had me wrapped around the axle?

How can I learn from this and move on easier?
What will I learn from this so it never happens again? (OOH. I just love this one.) What will I put into place based on what I learned so that it's different next time?

Ok. Seriously. I know that's more than one question for my last, best, and favorite of all time.

To start, learning is the only thing you need to remember. When you get the learning, the emotion can die down and you get your instant reset. Nice, huh?

That's the end of the list... for now.

Which questions are your favorites? What questions are you going to add?

WHEN I GET THE LEARNING

When I get the learning,
I can let go the negative emotions.
I am still learning.
I am learning how to be.
I am learning how to joy.
I am learning how to peace.
I am learning how to live.
I am being taught...
When I get the learning.

It Takes Grace and Courage

Burning out isn't fun.

Burning out wrecks your life.

I get it. I've been there. No joy.

Do something different.

Get the tools.

Use the tools.

Rock your confidence.

I pray grace and courage for you.

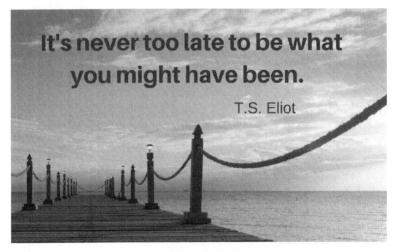

It's never too late to be what you might have been.

T.S. Eliot

It takes grace and courage...
To love in the midst of hatred.
To joy in the midst of pain.
To delight as a way to punctuate the sorrow.

It takes grace and courage...
To admit that I've been wrong.
To be willing to admit defeat: that I can't do it all after all.
To admit that I've thought myself a failure.

It takes grace and courage...
To be willing to forgive, even if I can't seem to right now.
To be aware of the wound so that the healing can begin.
To forgive those who didn't protect me.
To be willing to forgive... myself.

It takes grace and courage...
To reach out to the one that is most usually tucked in the farthest corners of a darkened, hardened, guarded heart. Me. I choose me.

It takes grace and courage...
To be willing to open up when it's safe.
To love myself and who I am at my core.

It takes grace and courage...
To begin again.
To take that first step...
*   ...and the next... and the next...*

It takes grace and courage…
To get back up after I stumble and fall.
To help another rise again.

It takes grace and courage…
To have patience and care.
To be grateful, in spirt of and even though.
To invite life again.

It takes grace and courage…
To ask the powerful questions –
What helped in the past, but doesn't serve me anymore?
What can I let go of?
What shall I grab onto?
How will I grow from this?
How can I be thankful?
What is the impact that I was built to make?

In the end, I invite, welcome, accept and receive
Grace and Courage now.

Rich, gorgeous, brilliant
blessings on your journey.

Love, *ANA-CHRISTINA*

**Action has magic,
grace, and power in it.**
Goethe

**Though I may sit in darkness,
You will be my light;
though I have fallen,
I will rise.**
Inspired by Micah 7:8

Because you got to the end of the book, it means you are dedicated to taking action. Taking action means that you are dedicated to change and growth.

Congratulations. You rock.

Thank you for what you do to help others.

Acknowledgements

As far as I'm concerned, you can never say thank you enough to those who have truly touched you, taught you, listened through the darkness, laughed and celebrated through the triumph, kept your heart safe, and loved you unconditionally. You can keep trying though...

To my extraordinary support system. You lift me up. You point me in the right direction—up and forward. Always. You encourage me. You allow me to join in on your journey. You make it safe to learn and grow and learn again.

To my amazing and generous editing team: Celeste, Jim, Laura, and Susan. Thank you for your time and heart. You helped me clarify thoughts, ideas, and untangle some knots. It's clearer, cleaner, and stronger because of you. Here's to simple.

To my parents, Gloria and Sal, some of the most selfless and generous hearts I know. I am privileged to be your daughter. To my sisters, Alissa, Tania, Laura, and Teressa. The Varela girls. I love you dearly.

A special shout out to my sons—you have helped me be strong. You have my heart—Colin, Nicholas, Christopher and grandson, Marlow.

To my special prayer and praise warriors—Jim, Karen, Alicia, Gloria, Tania. Thank you. You lift me when I get tired. You encourage me to shine my light.

To Joyce—you consistently point me to my Rock for healing. Thank you for being a rock for me on this journey.

To my bond and my lighthouse—you not only keep me from banging into the rocks, warning me from running too fast, but you have helped me heal and live from such joy—my Wilson.

To my Lord and my God, my Fortress, my Rock, my Sun and my Shield. I thank You with all I am. May I return to You all that You have given to me. Thank You for the strength, joy, grace and hope.

Always Hope. Eph. 3:19-20. Yes and Amen.

CONTACT

Rock-solid confidence.
UpYourGame. RaiseYourHappy. GetYourLifeBack.
You can so do this. My passion is sharing tools &
resources. Want more? Book your consult call now.
Free. Fun. Fruitful. Get on the phone and chat.
hope@toolsofhope.com 720-984-1463
www.toolsofhope.com

Thank you for who you are and what you do. Bless
you in your work. *ANA-CHRISTINA*

1:1 Coaching: Get coaching. Get support. Get Results.
www.toolsofhope.com

Speaking / Training: Keynotes. Breakouts.
Resilience training to keep your team in the game.
Clients:
U.S. Department of the Interior / U.S. Navy / U.S. Air
Force / Colorado State University / DaVita / NOVA—
National Organization for Victim Assistance /
COVA—Colorado / Southern States Victim Assistance
Conference / ISCA—International Customer Service
Association / Help Desk International / Department of
Justice U.S. Attorney's Office—SSVAC / MADD—
Mothers Against Drunk Driving / Perfect Teeth / Vail
Mountain School / Nisqually Indian Tribe / Accusum /
RMWLE—Rocky Mtn Women in Law Enforcement /
Rocky Mtn Police Chaplains / Rocky Mtn. Hostage
Negotiators / Wyoming Criminal Justice Association /
Kaiser Permanente.

Books:

Single copies: Find us on Amazon.
Discount bulk orders of books: Contact me directly.

TOOLS OF HOPE
  Simple Tools to Restore and Renew

BURNOUT'S KRYPTONITE
  for the Female First Responder.

Contact me directly for additional tools:

Seeds of Hope: prayer and scripture cards for the
  broken, the lost, and the crushed.

Coming soon:

RESILIENCE SECRETS of a 911 Dispatch Professional –
  with Natalia Duran (interview format – get real tools
  from a 35-year pro.)

RESILIENCE SECRETS of a Female Law Enforcement
  Officer—with Fran Gomez (interview format—get real
  tools from a 30 year LEO veteran.)

Made in the USA
Columbia, SC
09 September 2019